D0828253

PHEW!
THE SKUNK
AND OTHER STINKY ANIMALS

Greg Roza

PowerKiDS press

New York

Published in 2011 by The Rosen Publishing Group, Inc.
29 East 21st Street, New York, NY 10010

First Edition

Editor: Jennifer Way
Book Design: Kate Laczynski

Photo Credits: Cover, pp. 1, 9, 20–21 Comstock/Thinkstock; p. 4 Daniel Cox/Getty Images; pp. 5 (top), 14, 16, 18 iStockphoto/Thinkstock; pp. 5 (bottom), 12, 17 Shutterstock.com; p. 6 Karl Weatherly/Photodisc/ Thinkstock; p. 7 Jack Milchanowski/Visuals Unlimited, Inc./Getty Images; p. 8 Tom Ulrich/Getty Images; p. 10 Frank Lukasseck/Getty Images; p. 11 Digital Vision/Thinkstock; p. 13 © www.iStockphoto.com/ Stephan Drescher; p. 15 (top) Jens Schlueter/AFP/Getty Images; p. 15 (bottom) © www.iStockphoto.com/ Adam Goss; p. 19 Flip De Nooyer/Foto Natura/Getty Images; p. 22 © www.iStockphoto.com/James Coleman.

Library of Congress Cataloging-in-Publication Data

Roza, Greg.
  Phew! : the skunk and other stinky animals / by Greg Roza. — 1st ed.
     p. cm. — (Armed and dangerous)
Includes index.
  ISBN 978-1-4488-2549-3 (library binding) — ISBN 978-1-4488-2682-7 (pbk.) —
ISBN 978-1-4488-2683-4 (6-pack)
  1. Skunks—Juvenile literature. 2. Odors—Juvenile literature. 3. Animal defenses—Juvenile literature. I. Title.
  QL737.C248R69 2011
  591.47—dc22

                               2010025762

Manufactured in the United States of America

C⸺ Compliance Information: Batch #WW11PK: For Further Information contact Rosen Publishing, New York, New York at 1-800-237-9932

CONTENTS

THAT STINKS!

In the wild, staying alive depends on an animal's skill at **defending** itself. Some animals use sharp teeth and claws to scare away enemies. Other animals use their speed to get away. Other animals have weirder ways of defending themselves. Some animals are so stinky they scare away their enemies!

Skunks have special organs called scent glands under their tails. These glands make the stinky spray the animal uses as a defense.

Stinkbugs have scent glands on the undersides of their bodies. They use their stink to make predators go away.

Have you ever smelled something so bad that you just wanted to get away from it? Imagine if that bad smell was sprayed all over you! This is how **predators** learn to stay away from stinky animals like skunks.

There are even stinky snakes! This fox snake has scent glands near the end of its body that let out a bad smell.

MAKING A STINK

Not many animals use bad smells to defend themselves. Those that do, however, all have small body parts called scent **glands**. These glands make special liquids that are often called musk. In **mammals**, the musk gland is commonly found under their tails.

Some animals, such as deer and foxes, use their musk to draw **mates** to

Many animals, such as deer, have scent glands that they use to draw mates to them.

them. This type of musk is stinky, but it does not smell too bad or too strong. The skunk, on the other hand, makes a musk that smells so bad and so strong that it scares predators away. When a skunk feels **threatened**, it turns, lifts its tail, and sprays!

SMELLY SKUNKS

The skunk is the animal best known for its stinky defense. There are several kinds of skunks, including striped, spotted, and hog-nosed skunks. Most skunks have black fur with white stripes or spots. Skunks make their stink with two large musk glands under their tails. Skunk musk is more commonly called skunk spray.

There are 10 kinds of skunks in the world. This is a spotted skunk. Spotted skunks live in North America.

Skunks do not hide when trouble is around. When a skunk feels threatened, its tail goes straight up. That is a sign to predators to get out of the way or get sprayed! Skunks can spray their stinky musk up to 12 feet (4 m) away!

STINK AND STING

Skunk spray does not just stink. It stings the eyes and can cause blindness for a short time! It sends predators away gagging. Skunk spray is also hard to wash off, so a predator will have a reminder of its run-in with a skunk for several days.

Skunks rest in burrows. They either dig these burrows with their sharp front claws or look for a space such as a hollow log.

Some predators, such as eagles and vultures, have a poor sense of smell. These animals will attack skunks even after being sprayed. Great horned owls' nests are known to smell like skunk spray. This is because great horned owls are one of the few predators that will kill and eat skunks.

WHAT'S IN SKUNK SPRAY?

Skunk spray is made up mostly of two types of **chemicals**. One type makes a very bad smell. The chemicals in this type include sulfur. Sulfur is added to natural gas so people can smell gas leaks. It is also the chemical that makes rotten eggs smell bad!

This little bear might get a stinky surprise if it does not back away from this skunk! If the bear gets sprayed, it will smell bad for a few days and will likely stay away from skunks for the rest of its life.

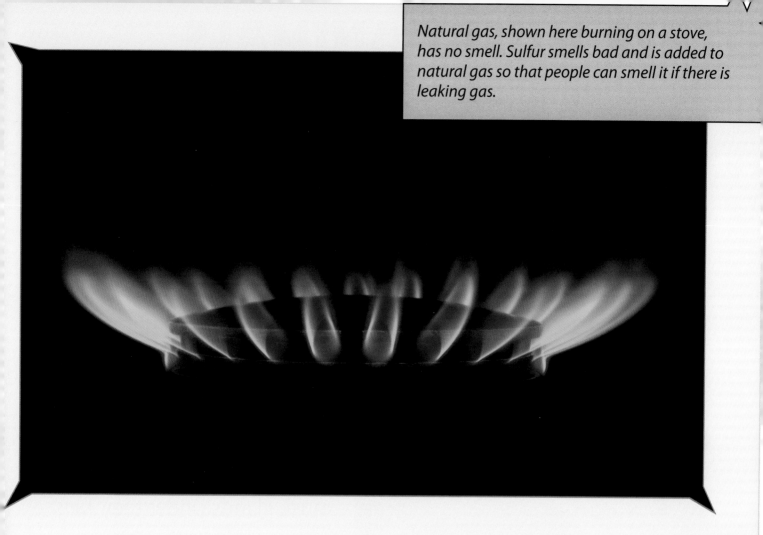

Natural gas, shown here burning on a stove, has no smell. Sulfur smells bad and is added to natural gas so that people can smell it if there is leaking gas.

The other type of chemical is an oily liquid that makes the bad odor stick to animals. This liquid makes it hard to wash off skunk spray. This is why animals that have been sprayed sometimes smell skunky long after they have been sprayed.

OTHER MUSKY ANIMALS

Weasels, mink, and ferrets are members of a family of musk-making animals called Mustelidae. They are called mustelids. Skunks were once thought to be members of this family. They have since been named to their own scientific family, though. Just like skunks, mustelids have large musk glands under their tails. Many mustelids use their musk to draw mates to them and to mark their territories.

The European polecat, shown here, is another member of the Mustelidae family.

Mink, shown here, are mustelids that are known for their soft fur.

The musk glands in mustelids are smaller than skunks' musk glands. Mustelids also cannot spray musk, as skunks can. Even so, other animals find mustelids like the polecat and the stink badger smelly enough that they stay away from them.

Ferrets, like the one shown here, are popular household pets.

STINKBUGS

What do you call a bug that stinks? A stinkbug, of course! Stinkbugs are sometimes called shield bugs because they have hard, flat backs that look like shields. There are thousands of kinds of stinkbugs living all over the world.

Stinkbugs have two glands that make a stinky liquid. These glands are on the stinkbug's **thorax**. They

The hard, flat backs of stinkbugs has earned them the nickname shield bugs.

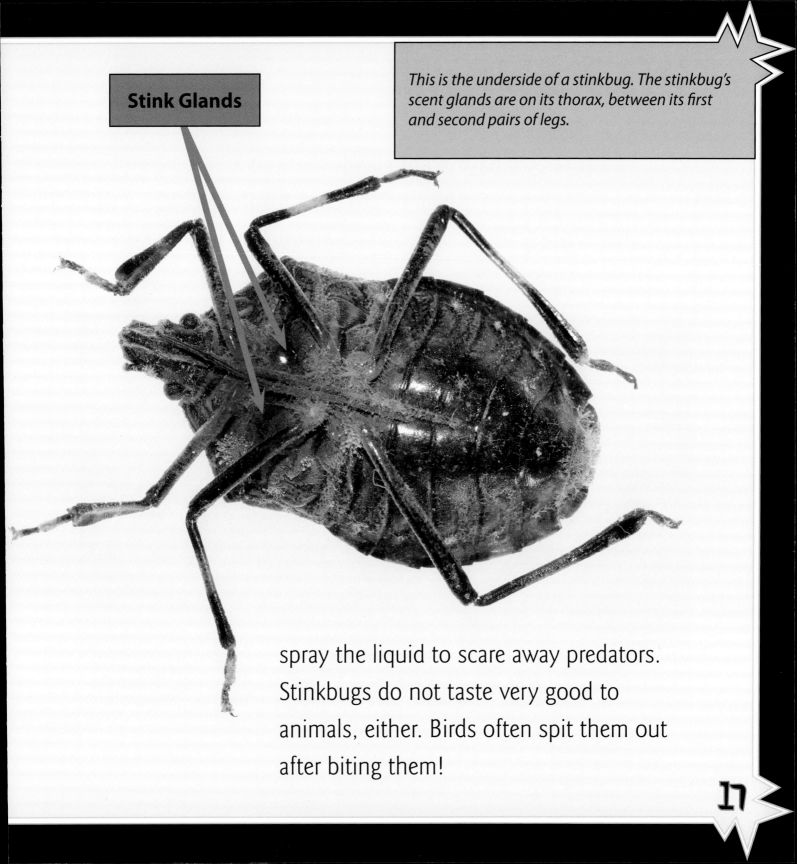

Stink Glands

This is the underside of a stinkbug. The stinkbug's scent glands are on its thorax, between its first and second pairs of legs.

spray the liquid to scare away predators. Stinkbugs do not taste very good to animals, either. Birds often spit them out after biting them!

STINKY SNAKES

Most snakes have scent glands that produce a musky smell. Snakes use their musk to **communicate** with other snakes. Some snakes make an odor so bad that it chases predators away. Others use their bad odor as

Garter snakes, like the one shown here, use scent to communicate. They also have a bad scent that they let out when they feel threatened by a predator.

a warning sign that they are ready to defend themselves with their teeth.

In the United States, the garter snake and the fox snake are known to spray bad-smelling musk when handled by people. Outside the United States, the European grass snake is well known for its stinky defense.

FUN FACTS

1 Some skunks drum their paws on the ground to warn away predators before spraying.

2 Spotted skunks are known to do handstands to make themselves look bigger to predators.

3 Skunks can even spray predators while upside down!

4 Some people have kept skunks as pets! This is not a good idea because they can carry illnesses.

The scientific name for the skunk family is Mephitidis. This comes from the Latin word for "bad smell."

5

The Mustelidae family has 54 different animals, including ferrets, badgers, otters, mink, and wolverines.

6

The zorilla, or striped polecat, is a mustelid that lives in Africa. In Sudan it is called the father of stinks!

7

One type of stinkbug can shoot a stinky liquid up to 1 foot (30 cm) away.

8

GET THE STINK OUT!

Skunks kill and eat pests such as mice, rats, roaches, and beetles. Sometimes a person or pet is unlucky enough to surprise a skunk. A skunk's oily musk can stick to the skin and stay around for days!

Soap and water are not enough to get rid of the skunk's smell. People once thought bathing in tomato juice got rid of the smell, but that is not true. Health experts say bathing in a mix of hydrogen peroxide, baking soda, and dish detergent will get rid of the smell. Of course, staying away from stinky animals is your best defense!

GLOSSARY

chemicals (KEH-mih-kulz) Matter that can be mixed with other matter to cause changes.

communicate (kuh-MYOO-nih-kayt) To share facts or feelings.

defending (dih-FEND-ing) Guarding from being hurt.

glands (GLANDZ) Organs or body parts that produce elements to help with bodily functions.

mammals (MA-mulz) Warm-blooded animals that have backbones and hair, breathe air, and feed milk to their young.

mates (MAYTS) Male and female animals that come together to make babies.

predators (PREH-duh-terz) Animals that kill other animals for food.

thorax (THOR-aks) The middle part of the body of an insect. The wings and legs are on the thorax.

threatened (THREH-tund) Acted as though something will possibly cause hurt.

INDEX

WEB SITES

Due to the changing nature of Internet links, PowerKids Press has developed an online list of Web sites related to the subject of this book. This site is updated regularly. Please use this link to access the list:
www.powerkidslinks.com/armd/phew/